L.R. has suffered through her life with depression and anxiety. Her coping mechanisms were to write out her thoughts and feelings onto paper, which soon turned into poetry. She has gone through the trials of pain, lust, hate, and love all throughout her teenage years. Her only dream was to become a writer and help those feeling alone or those suffering from mental illness. L.R. doesn't want anyone to feel alone through their tough times.

My loving mother who has supported in everything I chose. My stepdad, who took me in and treated me like a father should have. My future husband for helping me with everyday life.

My friend who I treat as my son.

L.R.

Fixator of the Broken

Austin Macauley Publishers™
London • Cambridge • New York • Sharjah

Ordering Information:
Quantity sales: special discounts are available on quantity purchases by corporations, associations, and others. For details, contact the publisher at the address below.

Publisher's Cataloging-in-Publication data
L.R.
Fixator of the Broken

ISBN 9781645753858 (Paperback)
ISBN 9781645753865 (Hardback)
ISBN 9781645753872 (ePub e-book)

www.austinmacauley.com/us

First Published (2020)
Austin Macauley Publishers LLC
40 Wall Street, 28th Floor
New York, NY 10005
USA

mail-usa@austinmacauley.com
+1 (646) 5125767

I would like to acknowledge my favorite writers, Rupi Kaur, E.H., Nikkita Gill, Emily Dickinson, Atticus, and R. H. Sin, for my writing styles and for inspiring me to become who I am today.

I want to mend the broken hearts,
I want to fix your broken soul,
With that feeling of not being alone,
Hoping you won't blow the candle out,
Because I am here,
Through this poetry,
And all this ink,

My veins filled with the alcohol that rushed down my throat. The thought of it being my only friend. I don't have a favorite cup, I have a favorite bottle.
My favorite spot to sleep is on the floor from passing out.
My favorite person to be with is the one living in my head.
My favorite shirt to wear is the one I can find the next day after throwing up on my last one.
My favorite medicine to cure the hangover is another bottle of whiskey.
My favorite heartache solution is another bottle of wine.
My favorite thing to not cure but mask my pain is another bottle of my only friend.
The thing that cures my headache is some aspirin with only a single bottle of rum.

The vodka bottle broke his teeth.
The smoke rolled through his nose.
The needle shot through his veins.
The tears stained his face.
The scars all over his legs.
The lies that whisper in his ear.
The ache in the chest felt like a punch.
The hammer pounded in his head.

The pills that sit in the beautiful white bottle across from him.
The thoughts weighing down him.
Suffocating.
He is tired. He can't take it.
The pills slipped down his throat with the bottle of whiskey that he found.
It started getting darker, and darker, through his bright blue eyes.
The pain started to slowly fade away from him.
The light in his eyes were gone.
He lay there, motionless.
The pills, alcohol, and the needle won.

The Pills sound like a siren.
The bottle of Vodka whistles.
The Pistol is tapping its barrel.
The knife is dancing on my arm.
My phone is buzzing.
I want my pain to stop.
I want my head to stop talking.
I want my body to stop aching.
I want my voice to stop cracking.
I want my lips to stop moving.
I want my eyes to stop crying.
I want my lungs to stop breathing.
I want my heart to stop beating.
'Boom'

Eyes rolled back,
Blood dripping from my head.

My body sat, motionless.
The vodka spilled.
The knife is covered in blood.
The pills spilled all over the floor.

The heart will remember what you did and choose to forgive you.
But my sweetheart, you will not hurt me.
I am colder than freezing.
I will not allow you to hurt me.
But you will not forget me.
I will leave a mark on your heart to the point, it will leave a scar.
I will take you all around to places you have never seen.
I will wrap your heart around my finger and take control of you until I decide when you are ready to feel my pain and understand me better than I understand myself.
I will take you on a journey through the hell I've been through, and decide when it is time to stop. If I deem you unworthy then trust me, I will drop and move on.
I have learned, I do not need anyone in my life because people come and go.
Only the ones that stay, are the ones that I have decided to let in.
So sweetie always remember.
It's not me, it is you.

Lost

She tries to stand, her addiction of him is now gone.
She drowned in her own tears.
She felt so useless.
All of her is numb
She stopped eating,
Thinking,
Believing,
Caring,
She's suffocating in the lies and betrayal.
She's waiting for the light to come back, but even that has given up on her.
She's searching for that last bit of hope…
The last bit of strength within her…

The canvas, the brush, and the paint.
There it lies in the hidden depths of my head.
The only brush i use,
To paint these beautiful pictures,
With this dark red paint,
On this canvas so small.
Helping release the pain i have felt.
But the brush wasn't a brush,

The canvas wasn't just a canvas,
The paint wasn't just paint.

The End

This is it,
The light at the end of the tunnel is glowing for me,
The last little happiness to seek inside,
My last breath must be taken from me,
The last bit of light to leave my eyes,
The last tear fallen from me,
No more scars to rise,
My last ounce of pain, gone, away from me,
No more devil,
No more shine,
This is it.
This is the end for me.

The thought of you sends chills through my spine.
I flinch at your name.
I ache at the thought of you.
You used to be my everything and now…we are nothing.
The pain I felt on my arm because the chaos in my head would not leave.
The thought of you makes me stagger back and fall on the floor.

I lay there on the cold, hard, concrete floor, rethinking the decisions I made.

With hair in my face and tears running out of my eyes, I wonder.

Was I not good enough for him?

I wonder how I managed to stay alive.

But I wasn't alive, simply surviving,

It killed me day by day.

It's like I shot the heroine through my veins that made me feel great at one point.

I knew you were not good for me but at the time you were.

Now I have withdrawn.

You.

The tears I can't escape from.

They rush down and will not stop multiplying.

They race each other to see who will come first.

First comes the thoughts.

Running round and round until they break into a sweat.

Then they need to cool off so they run out through my red eyes.

My eyes get this burning sensation because the thoughts take a dip in boiling water before breaking through the thought of me not crying.

They are salty when they hit my lip and arm. But then I look at my arm and imagine painting on them.

Then I stop imagining.

I slice in a slow movement across my arm.

I use the ridged side to make it seem easier.

I watch the blood start to spot up on my arm.

I take the brush and make a heart.

I remember just then that my heart was shattered.

So I slice it through the center.

The alcohol smell lingers on my breath.
The cigarette smell on my hoodie.
The blood running down my arm.
The thoughts chasing through.
The pills slip down my throat.
My smile fades.
My tears stop.
My heart slows down.
My eyes start to close.
I'm gone.

Depression

A monster.
This monster lives within me
Slowly pulling me down just below the surface.
I can see the light but it is just one, big, blur.
Sinking deeper. The monster growing stronger.
The light starting to fade.
The darkness consuming my own being.
No control.
The little ray of light grows more and more faint.
I am drowning
Water filling my lungs with every breath
A vine wrapped around my very own foot.
I can't swim to the waters break.
I can't breathe.

Time ticks on.
We want it to stop.
We think that the bottle of drugs and alcohol will speed up our death date.
We believe time heals all wounds.
Wrong.
Time does nothing but tick.

We heal our own wounds.
We speed up our death.
Not time.
For we are in control of our actions.
Time merely guides us along to keep us 'on the right track'.
But we will never know the right track.
Time will never force us to end our life.
We make that decision.
We make the decision to let the pills slip down our throats.
Not time.

She intoxicates herself to the point of delusion.
She lets the drink make her have a new idea of life.
She sits and sits like that's her life duty.
The thoughts she thinks will give her bad feelings, so she sips some more.
She emptied her cup but fills it right back up to hide away from the pain.
When the drinking stopped being enough, she found the sparkling white powder and sniffed.
She found the long needle and stuck it in her arm feeling higher than the clouds at this point.
Her pupils unable to focus.
She laid on the bed deathly still.
The alcohol on her breath.
The needle still in her arm.
The white sparkling powder sitting in a ring around her nose.
She believed that her purpose has been lost in the deep seas surrounding her.
The light was faded from her eyes.

Her heart was a slow, steady beat.
Her heart had come to a stop and the light from her eyes left and memories flashed.
She had finally given up.

This feeling inside me.
The unfiltered words coming out of my mouth.
The dangerous thoughts roaming in my head.
The feelings in my empty heart.
The things being dropped on my bottomless soul.
All coming together to start a war.
These come and make me stop eating, just to have the right body.
At the same time, making me binge eat without a second thought.
The emptiness in my stomach feels like there is something stuck in my throat and in between my rib cage.
The feeling of something scraping the bottom of your stomach.
This feeling I am now addicted to.
The feelings through my scrambled head and warm heart have started this war and right now my head is winning.
It has stopped me eating.
My heart still fights because I can still feel the love coming my way but very lightly it hits.
My mind has taken control my moods and does not let me see clearly.
Every once in a while, my heart packs a good punch but the mind heals so quickly it barely shows.
My heart cannot win this fight because it takes years of healing. My heart doesn't have years… It only has minutes.

My heart is covered in black ash and soot from all the fires that have burned on my heart. There are cracks that the gold seeps through. My heart is burning with the passion I carry. I have all this passion but only get burned. The happiness that once filled my heart and soul has now turned into sadness that lingers covering my body and heart with water. I drown for this. My Heart beats but only with hurt and loneliness. I let these people hold my heart and slowly squeeze the life out of it, only for me to refill it. The pain that swallows my heart is the black ash that sits on top slowly soaking into the inside of me. It is one big life cycle that goes round and round until finally my heart stops beating.

Think about it. Do the teachers see the cracks that lie in your eyes when you walk down the hallway staring at the floor? Do they notice when your gaze goes from them to the far side of the room and the thoughts are invading your mind? Do they notice the grades that start to fall and you start to lose focus? Do they notice when we start missing more and more days just to stay home and wallow in ourselves? Do they notice the lack of friends and confidence we have in every move we make? How our eyes scan the room to see if anyone is looking?

Alex was a boy that told me everything. Secrets, passions, hates, everything. We would play, laugh and go to his practices. His mom would attempt to talk to me though. His mom always asked who he was talking to when I was sitting right there. She always told Alex he needed some friends, but when he pointed to me, she would give him a cringe smile and say, okay. I never spoke to anyone but him. He started getting older and he started telling me less and less. His real friends started hanging out with him and he started telling them his secrets. Girls got in the way too. He started ignoring me. I can't complain too much. This is what happens to imaginary friends, right?

I didn't know not to trust you. I didn't know you would be like this. I was blinded by your words. They were like a blanket that covered me from all the bad things about you. You lead me to believe that you were some kind of angel but outside your twisted sweet words you were this demon that was taking everything around me away. I thought you were my sunshine but only when you would hide me under your blanket of words. Everything around me was dark and gloomy.

I have concealed my emotions with the makeup I put on my face. I hide everything behind these pained eyes and broken smile. I cover my body with a full cover to hide the fact that I'm not like all the skinny girls I wished to be. I do my hair to where I look mature, hoping they don't look at me like a joke. My family is falling apart, so I glue it back together with the glue I found in the bottom of the trash lying beside my hopes and dream.

You Said It

It took the breath out of my lungs and I stopped breathing.
My heart stopped beating for you once you said that.
I don't look to my past anymore but you rolled it up like a piece of paper and threw it right in my face like a joke.
That hit me hard, especially since you stopped talking to me.
You became a ghost for those two days and yet, I was the bad guy.
She ignored me like I was a ghost.
She then brings out the equipment to find me guilty of murder.
She puts me in a jar and shook it to make me release a sorry that she does not deserve.
She says she will leave this earth to get rid of her pain in which she inflicts on herself.
She twists his words to make her look good but yet doesn't know she does it.
She sits back and threatens her life to him.
She then comes to me but my words seem to be whispers in the wind and just do not seem to stick like snow to the trees.

This pain that is brewing inside me feels like knives digging into my heart and chest.
Slowly pushing deeper and deeper within me.
Over all these scars that keep getting re-opened.
There is no way to escape this pain any longer.
I can't hide this for much longer.
It pains me to see him with her.
I know I'm selfish and I can't seem to be the child he has ever wanted but now he has done so much damage I don't want to see him.
I don't want to face him.
He has dug that sword right in the center of my chest just because she wanted him to.
He has totally consumed himself in her.
She has him wrapped around her finger like a shark and it prey.
There is no getting away now.
She acts like she is my friend when really, she is using me.
She wants to gain my trust back but it will never happen again.
She is capable of so much and I'm the only one to see that.
She has manipulated everyone just for her sake.
The pain they are creating is getting worse and worse.
I can feel it eating me alive like a parasite.
I can't keep trying to balance all of this.
I know I'm strong but my strength is slipping in my fingertips.
I don't know how much farther I can go.

That girl that was made fun of for acne.
She thought about it every day and didn't show her face.

That girl that was bigger than everyone.
She starved herself.
That girl that was always so mean.
She had been hurt by too many people to feel.
That girl that was 'rich' and 'got what she wanted'.
She never asked for much.
That girl that thought school was going to be fun.
Was brought down by everyone.
That girl that actually believed in happiness.
She can't even smile anymore.
That girl that kept hurting but never showed.
She cried herself to sleep every night because of it.

She has this sparkle in her eyes that make my day glow bright. When she laughs it's like letting all my endorphins in my head out to make me feel. When she asks me about my day, I just want to hug her. When she hugs me, it's as if i can't get any closer. When we kiss, I feel tingly and a joy inside me that is like no other. When I look in those bright blue eyes, it's like the world just stops. It's like time itself has frozen. I could look into her beautiful bright blue eyes forever. She accepts me for who I am. She wants to take in all my flaws and the monster living within. She wants to see me. She makes me feel needed. She makes me feel wanted. When we touch it's like a thousand bolts of electricity go through me. She makes me want to love instead of hate.
She makes me want to succeed and not fail. I don't want to lose her. I can't lose her or my world will crash down into the fire. Her kiss still lingers on my lips when I leave. I crave the attention from her. I crave the thought of her laying down beside me holding me close. She is so beautiful in her

own way. Her smile she hides from the world. Her giggle that sends my mind into the clouds is what I crave to hear every waking moment. I may not be good at love poems but she makes me want to write about the feelings of love she gives me. She keeps my world spinning round and round. I hate seeing her cry and her blues eyes turn red. I want to take all the pain from her. I want her happy.

It's getting bad again,
It hasn't been like this in a while.
I start to zone,
My body starts to tense,
My face starts clenching,
Teeth start grinding,
My lungs start to work harder,
My anxiety is bad again,
I'm just sad.

I start to ramble,
About my life,
About my music,
About my pain,
About my happiness,
These thoughts swirl in my head,
I wonder why I live,
I ponder why I breathe,
Then I know,
I am the 'Fixator of the Broken'.

I want to mend the broken hearts,
I want to fix your broken soul,
With that feeling of not being alone,
Hoping you won't blow the candle out,
Because I am here,
Through this poetry,
And all this ink,

The pills sit in his bag,
Tempting him to take one,
The alcohol in his fridge,
Begs him to take some,
The knife tapping,
Asking to play a game.

His thoughts scratching his mind,
His hands cover his face,
The tears started running,
His eyes are playing peek a boo behind his hands,

The safest place there is,
Is in a bookstore.
With a cup of your favorite coffee,
Writing,
Reading,
Just to take some edge off,
Of the reality of this shitty world.

The sadness filling my heart,
The heavy brick on shoulders,
The dark cloud above my head,

The shake in my hands, the numb feeling in my legs
We call this depression.

They tell me to smile,
        I say okay.
They tell me not to lie,
        I say okay.
They tell me not to cry,
        I say okay.
They tell me to leave,
        I say okay.
They tell me to eat,
        I say okay.
They tell me to do this,
        I say okay.
They tell me not to do that,
        I say okay.
Do I listen?
No!

The dark cloud that pours the rain makes everything flood.
I'm sinking in the mud.
My hair is knotty like the mess in my head.
My clothes stick to me like my depression.
And the rain falls on me like the tears down my face.

This Is for You

The broken heart,
The nocturnal creature,
The abnormal eating habits,
The smell of whiskey on your breath,
The scars on your arm,
          This is for you
You are loved,
You are needed,
You are not alone,
You have a purpose,
          Stay strong.

Imagine

You're walking through a forest,
The wind is hard and cold,
Your feet in the mud,
The rain is like hail,
There is no light around you,
Trees are losing their leaves,
No other creature in sight,
Dark, lonely, scary.
That's my mind

I am a dock.
People are ships.
I let the dock for when they need me.
I give them whatever they need.
I'm always left empty until restocked.
Except the few that crash into my harbor,

Making me weak.

I am tired,
All I do is sleep,
I relax and stay unmoving,

I have no motivation,
My perfume is of my despair,
My clothes wrinkled,
My breath smells of procrastination,
My eyes saying I'm lonely,
My hands covered in dried tears,
I lay in my bed and shut my eyes that are heavy with pain.

The flowers start to bloom,
One bloomed earlier than the rest,
It was given a special serum,
Making it more fragile,
You need more water,
More fertilizer,
Learning to survive quicker,
All the other flowers are vibrant,
This one is dull.

The smile I wear on my face. My teeth shining in the sun. My hair gently blowing in the wind. The breeze tickling my ears. The freshness of the earth filling my nose. Looking at the different shades of color. Clouds passing by saying, hello. The dark cloud finally lifted. Happiness in my veins; I am free.

Fear. What is fear? It's like a dog on a leash. Getting walked by their owner. The owner controls where the dog goes. In this case, we are the dogs.

Free your soul,
Do what you love,
Smile at silly things,
Regret nothing,
Live your own life.

Pain
Compassion
Sadness
Happiness
Anger
Content
All factors of love.

With each pen stroke,
I think of you.
But on this page it was blank,
The I knew,
You were nothing to me.

You've always been there,
You've been hard on me,
You've pushed me to my limits,
You've noticed everything about me,
You've taught me so much,
You've treated me good and bad,
You've not always done what was right,
But you are still here,
You are me,
I am you.

Love isn’t always a good feeling,
There’s pain and hurt,
Bickering and fighting,
But…
There’s happiness and passion,
Laughing and smiling,
Loves isn’t the best,
But it can be.

You sweetie

Your eyes will get heavy,
Your heart will ache with heaviness,
Your hands will tremble,
Your stomach will turn,
Your face will burn,
Your head will hurt,
Your knees will give out,
It's called heartbreak.

Words are like venom,
Nothing happens at first,
But they kill you.

I miss him;
His smile,
His laugh,
His voice,
His words,
His compassion,
Everything…
But he's not thinking of me.

Look at them,
No, really, look!
Can you see it?
The smile slowly fading,
Their eyes scanning the room,
The skin chewed off by their nails,
The shaking in their body,
Look at them,
No, really, look!
Can you see it?

The look at their phone to break the awkwardness,
Their hands rubbing hard together,
Their words in a stutter,
Look at me,
No, don't!
You can't see.

Biting my lip as I look at you,
Nothing but chills run through my spine,
The goose bumps scatter over my skin,
My pupils dilate a slight bit bigger,
I brush the hair out of my blush face,
I look at you and smile.

You make me smile like a stormy night,
You make me want to stay in bed,
You make me want to rip my hair out,
You make me want to drink my life away,
I hate you!

Can you feel it?
That brick on your chest, made from thin air.
Can you see it?
The trickling blood coming from your arm?
Can you smell it?
The disappointment like perfume.
Can you hear it?
Sobs coming from your throat.
Can you taste it?
The salty tears on your lip.

Printed in the USA
CPSIA information can be obtained
at www.ICGtesting.com
LVHW021743301223
767736LV00005B/148

9 781645 753865